Y0-CCJ-272

DAYBREAK
PROMISES

for BELIEVERS

Titles in this series:

DAYBREAK
PROMISES

for BELIEVERS

Compiled by LARRY RICHARDS

ZONDERVAN®

ZONDERVAN

DayBreak Promises for Believers
Copyright © 2012 by Zondervan
All rights reserved

This title is also available as a Zondervan ebook.
Visit www.zondervan.com/ebooks.

Requests for information should be addressed to:

Zondervan, *Grand Rapids, Michigan* 49530

Library of Congress Catalog Card Number 2012939816

All Scripture quotations, unless otherwise indicated, are taken from the Holy Bible, *New International Version*®, *NIV*®. Copyright © 1973, 1978, 1984, 2011 by Biblica, Inc.™ Used by permission. All rights reserved worldwide.

Any Internet addresses (websites, blogs, etc.) and telephone numbers in this book are offered as a resource. They are not intended in any way to be or imply an endorsement by Zondervan, nor does Zondervan vouch for the content of these sites and numbers for the life of this book.

All rights reserved. No part of this publication may be reproduced, stored in a retrieval system, or transmitted in any form or by any means—electronic, mechanical, photocopy, recording, or any other—except for brief quotations in printed reviews, without the prior permission of the publisher.

Cover design: Jamie DeBruyn
Cover photography or illustration: istockphoto
Interior design: Nancy Wilson

Printed in the United States of America

---

12 13 14 15 16 17 18 /DPM/ 12 11 10 9 8 7 6 5 4 3 2 1

Your relationship with God through Jesus
is very close and very special.
This booklet will help you
sense it more deeply,
for it brings together his promises,
helping you grasp:
your very personal relationship with God;
God's promises for your times of need;
and special prayer and God's answers.

CONTENTS

INTRODUCTION

When you trusted Jesus Christ as your personal Savior, you became a member of God's family. You are His child now, through faith in Jesus (Galatians 3:26), and you are His special concern. You are also an inheritor of many wonderful promises. This booklet draws together great truths from the Old and the New Testament — truths that help you understand better God's commitment to you as His child.

There are three sections in this booklet, and in each section the verses are in random order, to avoid suggesting that a pattern of thought or teaching is being presented. The basic concept of this booklet is that Scripture provides a variety of insights for our particular needs, and that these insights should be allowed to stand on their own.

The first section in this booklet, "Your Very Personal Relationship With God," is filled with wonderful truths, truths containing promises that are now yours in Christ. When you feel uncertain, turn to this section and be refreshed by God's great love.

"God's Promises When You Are in Need" contains truths that speak to special needs. Perhaps you feel lonely, or discouraged. Perhaps you're sick, or nervous. Whatever your need, check the table of contents to find the page that shows you that God *does* care, and that He *will* care for you.

"Your Prayers . . . God's Answers" is filled with prayers uttered by Old and New Testament people and God's answers to their prayers. Prayer is one of your privileges as a member of God's family. You can share everything with God and be confident that He hears. This section will help you to express your feelings to God, and it will give you the assurance that God will answer you.

PART ONE

YOUR VERY PERSONAL RELATIONSHIP WITH GOD

When you committed yourself to Jesus, God made a deep commitment to you. You are his now, and he wants to make the unchanging nature of his commitment to you clear. He wants you to be confident, so that "we who have fled to take hold of the hope set before us may be greatly encouraged" (Hebrews 6:18).

LOVE

MATTHEW 10:30–31

"And even the very hairs of your head are all numbered. So don't be afraid; you are worth more than many sparrows."

EZEKIEL 34:31

"You are my sheep, the sheep of my pasture, and I am your God, declares the Sovereign LORD."

ISAIAH 43:1

But now, this is what the LORD says — he who created you, Jacob, he who formed you, Israel: "Do not fear, for I have redeemed you; I have summoned you by name; you are mine."

ISAIAH 54:10

"Though the mountains be shaken and the hills be removed, yet my unfailing love for you will not be shaken nor my covenant of peace be removed."

JEREMIAH 31:3–4

"I have loved you with an everlasting love; I have drawn you with unfailing kindness. I will build you up again, and you, Virgin Israel, will be rebuilt. Again you will take up your timbrels and go out to dance with the joyful."

EZEKIEL 36:9

"I am concerned for you and will look on you with favor; you will be plowed and sown."

PSALM 4:3

Know that the LORD has set apart his faithful servant for himself; the LORD hears when I call to him.

NAHUM 1:7

The LORD is good, a refuge in times of trouble. He cares for those who trust in him.

ZEPHANIAH 3:17

"The LORD your God is with you, the Mighty Warrior who saves. He will take great delight in you; in his love he will no longer rebuke you, but will rejoice over you with singing."

PSALM 57:3

He sends from heaven and saves me, rebuking those who hotly pursue me — God sends forth his love and his faithfulness.

PSALM 89:33

"I will not take my love from him, nor will I ever betray my faithfulness."

JOHN 3:16

For God so loved the world that he gave his one and only Son, that whoever believes in him shall not perish but have eternal life.

MALACHI 3:17

"On the day when I act," says the LORD Almighty, "they will be my treasured possession."

SALVATION

JOHN 1:12

To all who did receive him, to those who believed in his name, he gave the right to become children of God.

JOHN 3:36

Whoever believes in the Son has eternal life, but whoever rejects the Son will not see life, for God's wrath remains on them.

JOHN 5:24

"Very truly I tell you, whoever hears my word and believes him who sent me has eternal life and will not be judged but has crossed over from death to life."

JOHN 10:28

"I give them eternal life, and they shall never perish; no one will snatch them out of my hand."

Acts 16:31

"Believe in the Lord Jesus, and you will be saved — you and your household."

1 John 5:11–12

God has given us eternal life, and this life is in his Son. Whoever has the Son has life; whoever does not have the Son of God does not have life.

Hebrews 7:25

He is able to save completely those who come to God through him, because he always lives to intercede for them.

John 6:47

"Very truly I tell you, the one who believes has eternal life."

Ephesians 1:7

In him we have redemption through his blood, the forgiveness of sins, in accordance with the riches of God's grace.

Romans 10:11–13

As Scripture says, "Anyone who believes in him will never be put to shame." For there is no difference between Jew and Gentile — the same Lord is Lord of all and richly blesses all who call on him, for, "Everyone who calls on the name of the Lord will be saved."

FORGIVENESS

Psalm 85:2

You forgave the iniquity of your people and covered all their sins.

Psalm 86:5

You, Lord, are forgiving and good, abounding in love to all who call to you.

Psalm 103:3

[The Lord] forgives all your sins and heals all your diseases.

PSALM 103:12–14

As far as the east is from the west, so far has he removed our transgressions from us. As a father has compassion on his children, so the LORD has compassion on those who fear him; for he knows how we are formed, he remembers that we are dust.

PSALM 32:5–6

I acknowledged my sin to you and did not cover up my iniquity. I said, "I will confess my transgressions to the LORD." And you forgave the guilt of my sin. Therefore let all the faithful pray to you while you may be found; surely the rising of the mighty waters will not reach them.

JEREMIAH 31:34

"No longer will they teach their neighbor, or say to one another, 'Know the LORD,' because they will all know me, from the least of them to the greatest," declares the LORD. "For I will forgive their wickedness and will remember their sins no more."

1 JOHN 1:9

If we confess our sins, he is faithful and just and will forgive us our sins and purify us from all unrighteousness.

PSALM 86:5

You, Lord, are forgiving and good, abounding in love to all who call to you.

MICAH 7:18–19

Who is a God like you, who pardons sin and forgives the transgression of the remnant of his inheritance? You do not stay angry forever but delight to show mercy. You will again have compassion on us; you will tread our sins underfoot and hurl all our iniquities into the depths of the sea.

ACTS 10:43

"Everyone who believes in him receives forgiveness of sins through his name."

FREEDOM

JOHN 8:34–36

"Everyone who sins is a slave to sin. Now a slave has no permanent place in the family, but a son belongs to it forever. So if the Son sets you free, you will be free indeed."

ROMANS 6:20,22

When you were slaves to sin, you were free from the control of righteousness ... But now that you have been set free from sin and have become slaves of God, the benefit you reap leads to holiness, and the result is eternal life.

ROMANS 6:6

Our old self was crucified with him so that the body ruled by sin might be done away with, that we should no longer be slaves to sin.

ROMANS 6:14

Sin shall no longer be your master, because you are not under the law, but under grace.

EPHESIANS 2:4–7,10

Because of his great love for us, God, who is rich in mercy, made us alive with Christ even when we were dead in transgressions — it is by grace you have been saved. And God raised us up with Christ and seated us with him in the heavenly realms in Christ Jesus, in order that in the coming ages he might show the incomparable riches of his grace, expressed in his kindness to us in Christ Jesus ... For we are God's handiwork, created in Christ Jesus to do good works, which God prepared in advance for us to do.

1 JOHN 3:9

No one who is born of God will continue to sin, because God's seed remains in them; they cannot go on sinning, because they have been born of God.

ROMANS 1:16

The gospel . . . is the power of God that brings salvation to everyone who believes: first to the Jew, then to the Gentile.

_____GROWTH_____

2 CORINTHIANS 3:18

We all, who with unveiled faces contemplate the Lord's glory, are being transformed into his image with ever-increasing glory, which comes from the Lord, who is the Spirit.

PHILIPPIANS 1:6

Being confident of this, that he who began a good work in you will carry it on to completion until the day of Christ Jesus.

1 PETER 2:2–5

Like newborn babies, crave pure spiritual milk, so that by it you may grow up in your salvation, now that you have tasted that the Lord is good. As you come to him, the living Stone — rejected by humans but chosen by God and precious to him — you also, like living stones, are being built into a spiritual house to be a holy priesthood, offering spiritual sacrifices acceptable to God through Jesus Christ.

EPHESIANS 4:15–16

Speaking the truth in love, we will grow to become in every respect the mature body of him who is the head, that is, Christ. From him the whole body, joined and held together by every supporting ligament, grows and builds itself up in love, as each part does its work.

2 PETER 1:4–8

He has given us his very great and precious promises, so that through them you may participate in the divine nature, having escaped the corruption in the world caused by evil desires. For this very reason, make every effort to add to your faith goodness; and to goodness, knowledge; and to knowledge, self-control;

and to self-control, perseverance; and to perseverance, godliness; and to godliness, mutual affection; and to mutual affection, love. For if you possess these qualities in increasing measure, they will keep you from being ineffective and unproductive in your knowledge of our Lord Jesus Christ.

_____FAMILY_____

ISAIAH 63:16

You, LORD, are our Father, our Redeemer from of old is your name.

2 CORINTHIANS 6:18

"I will be a Father to you, and you will be my sons and daughters, says the Lord Almighty."

GALATIANS 3:26

In Christ Jesus you are all children of God through faith.

1 JOHN 2:23

Whoever acknowledges the Son has the Father also.

PSALM 103:13

As a father has compassion on his children, so the LORD has compassion on those who fear him.

JOHN 16:27

"The Father himself loves you because you have loved me and have believed that I came from God."

JOHN 20:17

Jesus said, "Do not hold on to me, for I have not yet ascended to the Father. Go instead to my brothers and tell them, 'I am ascending to my Father and your Father, to my God and your God.'"

HEBREWS 12:7–10

Endure hardship as discipline; God is treating you as his children. For what children are not disciplined by their father? If you are not disciplined — and everyone undergoes discipline — then you are not legitimate, not true sons and daughters at all. Moreover, we have all had human fathers who disciplined us and we respected them for it. How much more should we submit to the Father of spirits and live! They disciplined us for a little while as they thought best; but God disciplines us for our good, in order that we may share in his holiness.

JAMES 1:17

Every good and perfect gift is from above, coming down from the Father of the heavenly lights, who does not change like shifting shadows.

_____DISCIPLINE_____

JEREMIAH 30:11

" 'I am with you and will save you,' declares the LORD. 'Though I completely destroy all the nations among which I scatter you, I will not completely destroy you. I will discipline you but only in due measure; I will not let you go entirely unpunished.' "

DEUTERONOMY 8:5

Know then in your heart that as a man disciplines his son, so the LORD your God disciplines you.

HEBREWS 12:10

God disciplines us for our good, in order that we may share in his holiness.

HEBREWS 12:11

No discipline seems pleasant at the time, but painful. Later on, however, it produces a harvest of righteousness and peace for those who have been trained by it.

PSALM 94:12–14

Blessed is the one you discipline, LORD, the one you teach from your law; you grant them relief from days of trouble, till a pit is dug for the wicked. For the LORD will not reject his people; he will never forsake his inheritance.

PROVERBS 3:11–12

Do not despise the LORD's discipline, and do not resent his rebuke, because the LORD disciplines those he loves, as a father the son he delights in.

REVELATION 3:19

"Those whom I love I rebuke and discipline. So be earnest and repent."

1 CORINTHIANS 11:32

When we are judged in this way by the Lord, we are being disciplined so that we will not be finally condemned with the world.

PROVERBS 6:23

This command is a lamp, this teaching is a light, and correction and instruction are the way to life.

PROVERBS 13:24

Whoever spares the rod hates their children, but the one who loves their children is careful to discipline them.

HOLINESS

2 CORINTHIANS 5:21

God made him who had no sin to be sin for us, so that in him we might become the righteousness of God.

2 PETER 1:3

His divine power has given us everything we need for a godly life through our knowledge of him who called us by his own glory and goodness.

LEVITICUS 20:7–8

"Consecrate yourselves and be holy, because I am the LORD your God. Keep my decrees and follow them. I am the LORD, who makes you holy."

EPHESIANS 1:4

He chose us in him before the creation of the world to be holy and blameless in his sight.

Ephesians 5:25–27

Christ loved the church and gave himself up for her to make her holy, cleansing her by the washing with water through the word, and to present her to himself as a radiant church, without stain or wrinkle or any other blemish, but holy and blameless.

1 Thessalonians 3:13

May he strengthen your hearts so that you will be blameless and holy in the presence of our God and Father when our Lord Jesus comes with all his holy ones.

1 Thessalonians 4:3

It is God's will that you should be sanctified.

1 Timothy 6:18–19

Command them to do good, to be rich in good deeds, and to be generous and willing to share. In this way they will lay up treasure for themselves as a firm foundation for the coming age, so that they may take hold of the life that is truly life.

1 John 5:18

We know that anyone born of God does not continue to sin; the One who was born of God keeps them safe, and the evil one cannot harm them.

_____COMFORT_____

Psalm 46:7

The Lord Almighty is with us; the God of Jacob is our fortress.

Psalm 103:17

From everlasting to everlasting the Lord's love is with those who fear him, and his righteousness with their children's children.

Romans 8:38–39

For I am convinced that neither death nor life, neither angels nor demons, neither the present nor the future, nor any powers, neither height nor depth, nor anything else in all creation, will be able to separate us from the love of God that is in Christ Jesus our Lord.

NUMBERS 14:9

"The LORD is with us."

DEUTERONOMY 31:6

"Be strong and courageous. Do not be afraid or terrified because of them, for the LORD your God goes with you; he will never leave you nor forsake you."

PSALM 27:10

Though my father and mother forsake me, the LORD will receive me.

PSALM 73:23

I am always with you; you hold me by my right hand.

MATTHEW 28:20

"Surely I am with you always, to the very end of the age."

JOHN 6:37–39

"All those the Father gives me will come to me, and whoever comes to me I will never drive away. For I have come down from heaven not to do my will but to do the will of him who sent me. And this is the will of him who sent me, that I shall lose none of all those he has given me, but raise them up at the last day."

ISAIAH 41:17

"I the LORD will answer them; I, the God of Israel, will not forsake them."

PSALM 94:14

The LORD will not reject his people; he will never forsake his inheritance.

_____PROVISION_____

DEUTERONOMY 20:4

"The LORD your God is the one who goes with you to fight for you against your enemies to give you victory."

1 SAMUEL 17:47

"It is not by sword or spear that the LORD saves; for the battle is the LORD's."

DEUTERONOMY 10:21

He is the one you praise; he is your God, who performed for you those great and awesome wonders you saw with your own eyes.

PSALM 22:4–5

In you [God] our ancestors put their trust; they trusted and you delivered them. To you they cried out and were saved; in you they trusted and were not put to shame.

ISAIAH 40:28–29

Do you not know? Have you not heard? The LORD is the everlasting God, the Creator of the ends of the earth. He will not grow tired or weary, and his understanding no one can fathom. He gives strength to the weary and increases the power of the weak.

PSALM 77:14

You are the God who performs miracles; you display your power among the peoples.

ISAIAH 41:13

"For I am the LORD your God who takes hold of your right hand and says to you, Do not fear; I will help you."

1 SAMUEL 2:8–9

"He raises the poor from the dust and lifts the needy from the ash heap; he seats them with princes and has them inherit a throne of honor. For the foundations of the earth are the LORD's; on them he has set the world. He will guard the feet of his faithful servants."

ISAIAH 33:22

For the LORD is our judge, the LORD is our lawgiver, the LORD is our king; it is he who will save us.

_____PRAYER_____

MATTHEW 7:7

"Ask and it will be given to you; seek and you will find; knock and the door will be opened to you."

MATTHEW 7:8

"Everyone who asks receives; the one who seeks finds; and to the one who knocks, the door will be opened."

1 PETER 3:12

"The eyes of the Lord are on the righteous and his ears are attentive to their prayer."

JOHN 14:13

"I will do whatever you ask in my name, so that the Father may be glorified in the Son."

JOHN 14:14

"You may ask me for anything in my name, and I will do it."

1 JOHN 5:14–15

This is the confidence we have in approaching God: that if we ask anything according to his will, he hears us. And if we know that he hears us — whatever we ask — we know that we have what we asked of him.

PSALM 4:3

Know that the LORD has set apart his faithful servant for himself; the LORD hears when I call to him.

MATTHEW 7:9–11

"Which of you, if your son asks for bread, will give him a stone? Or if he asks for a fish, will give him a snake? If you, then, though you are evil, know how to give good gifts to your children, how much more will your Father in heaven give good gifts to those who ask him!"

PSALM 65:2,5

You who answer prayer, to you all people will come . . . You answer us with awesome and righteous deeds, God our Savior, the hope of all the ends of the earth and of the farthest seas.

ISAIAH 59:1

Surely the arm of the LORD is not too short to save, nor his ear too dull to hear.

GUIDANCE

EXODUS 15:13

In your unfailing love you will lead the people you have redeemed. In your strength you will guide them to your holy dwelling.

EXODUS 4:12

"I will help you speak and will teach you what to say."

ISAIAH 30:21

Whether you turn to the right or to the left, your ears will hear a voice behind you, saying, "This is the way; walk in it."

PROVERBS 2:6

The LORD gives wisdom; from his mouth come knowledge and understanding.

PSALM 32:8

I will instruct you and teach you in the way you should go; I will counsel you with my loving eye on you.

JOHN 14:26

"The Advocate, the Holy Spirit, whom the Father will send in my name, will teach you all things and will remind you of everything I have said to you."

JOB 32:8–9

"It is the spirit in a person, the breath of the Almighty, that gives them understanding. It is not only the old who are wise, not only the aged who understand what is right."

PSALM 73:24

You guide me with your counsel, and afterward you will take me into glory.

DEUTERONOMY 29:29

The secret things belong to the LORD our God, but the things revealed belong to us and to our children forever, that we may follow all the words of this law.

LUKE 21:15

"I will give you words and wisdom that none of your adversaries will be able to resist or contradict."

JOHN 16:13

"When he, the Spirit of truth, comes, he will guide you into all the truth. He will not speak on his own; he will speak only what he hears, and he will tell you what is yet to come."

STRENGTH

JOEL 2:29

"Even on my servants, both men and women, I will pour out my Spirit in those days."

JOHN 7:38–39

"Whoever believes in me, as Scripture has said, rivers of living water will flow from within them." By this he meant the Spirit, whom those who believed in him were later to receive. Up to that time the Spirit had not been given, since Jesus had not yet been glorified.

JOHN 14:16–17

I will ask the Father, and he will give you another advocate to help you and be with you forever — the Spirit of truth.

ROMANS 8:11

If the Spirit of him who raised Jesus from the dead is living in you, he who raised Christ from the dead will also give life to your mortal bodies because of his Spirit who lives in you.

1 CORINTHIANS 6:19

Your bodies are temples of the Holy Spirit, who is in you, whom you have received from God.

1 JOHN 4:4

The one who is in you is greater than the one who is in the world.

PSALM 29:11

The LORD gives strength to his people; the LORD blesses his people with peace.

PSALM 63:8

I cling to you; your right hand upholds me.

EPHESIANS 3:20

[God] is able to do immeasurably more than all we ask or imagine, according to his power that is at work within us.

PSALM 89:21

"My hand will sustain him; surely my arm will strengthen him."

ISAIAH 12:2

"Surely God is my salvation; I will trust and not be afraid. The LORD, the LORD himself, is my strength and my defense; he has become my salvation."

PROTECTION

PSALM 18:30

As for God, his way is perfect: The LORD's word is flawless; he shields all who take refuge in him.

PSALM 37:40

The LORD helps them and delivers them; he delivers them from the wicked and saves them, because they take refuge in him.

PSALM 91:14

"Because he loves me," says the LORD, "I will rescue him; I will protect him, for he acknowledges my name."

PSALM 116:6

The LORD protects the unwary; when I was brought low, he saved me.

PSALM 121:2–3

My help comes from the LORD, the Maker of heaven and earth. He will not let your foot slip — he who watches over you will not slumber.

JEREMIAH 31:28

"I will watch over them to build and to plant," declares the LORD.

PSALM 91:4

He will cover you with his feathers, and under his wings you will find refuge; his faithfulness will be your shield and rampart.

PSALM 91:9–10

If you say, "The LORD is my refuge," and you make the Most High your dwelling, no harm will overtake you, no disaster will come near your tent.

PSALM 31:23

Love the LORD, all his faithful people! The LORD preserves those who are true to him.

2 TIMOTHY 1:12

I know whom I have believed, and am convinced that he is able to guard what I have entrusted to him until that day.

PSALM 37:28

The LORD loves the just and will not forsake his faithful ones.

PSALM 12:7

You, LORD, will keep the needy safe and will protect us forever from the wicked.

CARE

2 CORINTHIANS 9:8

And God is able to bless you abundantly, so that in all things at all times, having all that you need, you will abound in every good work.

ISAIAH 58:11

"The LORD will guide you always; he will satisfy your needs in a sun-scorched land and will strengthen your frame. You will be like a well-watered garden, like a spring whose waters never fail."

DEUTERONOMY 8:10

When you have eaten and are satisfied, praise the LORD your God for the good land he has given you.

PSALM 23:1

The LORD is my shepherd, I lack nothing.

DEUTERONOMY 8:18

Remember the LORD your God, for it is he who gives you the ability to produce wealth, and so confirms his covenant, which he swore to your ancestors, as it is today.

PSALM 95:7

He is our God and we are the people of his pasture, the flock under his care.

PSALM 54:4

Surely God is my help; the Lord is the one who sustains me.

1 CHRONICLES 29:11–12

"Yours, LORD, is the greatness and the power and the glory and the majesty and the splendor, for everything in heaven and earth is yours. Yours, LORD, is the kingdom; you are exalted as head over all. Wealth and honor come from you; you are the ruler of all things. In your hands are strength and power to exalt and give strength to all."

Matthew 6:25–26

"Therefore I tell you, do not worry about your life, what you will eat or drink; or about your body, what you will wear. Is not life more than food, and the body more than clothes? Look at the birds of the air; they do not sow or reap or store away in barns, and yet your heavenly Father feeds them. Are you not much more valuable than they?"

Philippians 4:19

God will meet all your needs according to the riches of his glory in Christ Jesus.

OBEDIENCE

Jeremiah 31:33

"This is the covenant I will make with the people of Israel after that time," declares the LORD. "I will put my law in their minds and write it on their hearts. I will be their God, and they will be my people."

2 Corinthians 3:3

You are a letter from Christ, the result of our ministry, written not with ink but with the Spirit of the living God, not on tablets of stone but on tablets of human hearts.

Hebrews 9:14

How much more, then, will the blood of Christ, who through the eternal Spirit offered himself unblemished to God, cleanse our consciences from acts that lead to death, so that we may serve the living God!

Leviticus 9:6

"This is what the LORD has commanded you to do, so that the glory of the LORD may appear to you."

JOHN 14:21

"Whoever has my commands and keeps them is the one who loves me. The one who loves me will be loved by my Father, and I too will love them and show myself to them."

JOHN 14:23–24

"Anyone who loves me will obey my teaching. My Father will love them, and we will come to them and make our home with them. Anyone who does not love me will not obey my teaching."

1 JOHN 3:6

No one who lives in him keeps on sinning.

1 JOHN 5:3–5

This is love for God: to keep his commands. And his commands are not burdensome, for everyone born of God overcomes the world . . . Who is it that overcomes the world? Only the one who believes that Jesus is the Son of God.

PSALM 119:30–32

I have chosen the way of faithfulness; I have set my heart on your laws. I hold fast to your statutes, LORD; do not let me be put to shame. I run in the path of your commands, for you have broadened my understanding.

BLESSINGS

EZEKIEL 34:26

"I will send down showers in season; there will be showers of blessing."

ROMANS 8:32

He who did not spare his own Son, but gave him up for us all — how will he not also, along with him, graciously give us all things?

EPHESIANS 1:3

Praise be to the God and Father of our Lord Jesus Christ, who has blessed us in the heavenly realms with every spiritual blessing in Christ.

PSALM 31:19

How abundant are the good things that you have stored up for those who fear you, that you bestow in the sight of all, on those who take refuge in you.

PSALM 67:7

May God bless us still, so that all the ends of the earth will fear him.

PSALM 84:5

Blessed are those whose strength is in you, whose hearts are set on pilgrimage.

PSALM 85:12

The LORD will indeed give what is good, and our land will yield its harvest.

PSALM 107:9

He satisfies the thirsty and fills the hungry with good things.

PSALM 115:13

He will bless those who fear the LORD — small and great alike.

ISAIAH 3:10

Tell the righteous it will be well with them, for they will enjoy the fruit of their deeds.

PSALM 128:1

Blessed are all who fear the LORD, who walk in obedience to him.

JEREMIAH 17:7

"Blessed is the one who trusts in the LORD, whose confidence is in him."

PSALM 115:12

The LORD remembers us and will bless us.

JEREMIAH 32:40

I will never stop doing good to them.

REWARDS

JEREMIAH 17:10

"I the LORD search the heart and examine the mind, to reward each person according to their conduct."

MATTHEW 6:4

"So that your giving may be in secret. Then your Father, who sees what is done in secret, will reward you."

MATTHEW 19:28–29

"Truly I tell you, at the renewal of all things . . . everyone who has left houses or brothers or sisters or father or mother or wife or children or fields for my sake will receive a hundred times as much and will inherit eternal life."

JOHN 12:26

"Whoever serves me must follow me; and where I am, my servant also will be. My Father will honor the one who serves me."

COLOSSIANS 3:24

Since you know that you will receive an inheritance from the Lord as a reward. It is the Lord Christ you are serving.

2 TIMOTHY 4:8

Now there is in store for me the crown of righteousness, which the Lord, the righteous Judge, will award to me on that day — and not only to me, but also to all who have longed for his appearing.

2 SAMUEL 22:21

"The LORD has dealt with me according to my righteousness; according to the cleanness of my hands he has rewarded me."

1 PETER 1:3–5

In his great mercy he has given us new birth into a living hope through the resurrection of Jesus Christ from the dead, and into an inheritance that can never perish, spoil or fade. This inheritance is kept in heaven for you, who through faith are shielded by God's power until the coming of the salvation that is ready to be revealed in the last time.

1 PETER 5:4

When the Chief Shepherd appears, you will receive the crown of glory that will never fade away.

_____SERVICE_____

MATTHEW 5:9

Blessed are the peacemakers, for they will be called children of God.

MATTHEW 10:42

"If anyone gives even a cup of cold water to one of these little ones who is my disciple, truly I tell you, that person will certainly not lose their reward."

1 CORINTHIANS 12:7

Now to each one the manifestation of the Spirit is given for the common good.

1 SAMUEL 12:23

"As for me, far be it from me that I should sin against the LORD by failing to pray for you. And I will teach you the way that is good and right."

PSALM 41:1

Blessed are those who have regard for the weak; the LORD delivers them in times of trouble.

PSALM 112:5

Good will come to those who are generous and lend freely.

PROVERBS 19:17

Whoever is kind to the poor lends to the LORD, and he will reward them for what they have done.

JOB 6:14

"Anyone who withholds kindness from a friend forsakes the fear of the Almighty."

2 Corinthians 1:3–4

Praise be to the God . . . of all comfort, who comforts us in all our troubles, so that we can comfort those in any trouble with the comfort we ourselves receive from God.

2 Corinthians 3:5–6

Not that we are competent in ourselves to claim anything for ourselves, but our competence comes from God. He has made us competent as ministers of a new covenant.

1 Peter 4:10

Each of you should use whatever gift you have received to serve others, as faithful stewards of God's grace in its various forms.

FELLOWSHIP

Genesis 2:18,22

The Lord God said, "It is not good for the man to be alone. I will make a helper suitable for him." . . . Then the Lord God made a woman from the rib he had taken out of the man, and he brought her to the man.

Mark 12:31

"Love your neighbor as yourself."

John 13:34–35

"A new command I give you: Love one another. As I have loved you, so you must love one another. By this everyone will know that you are my disciples, if you love one another."

Romans 13:8

Let no debt remain outstanding, except the continuing debt to love one another, for whoever loves others has fulfilled the law.

Romans 15:5–6

May the God who gives endurance and encouragement give you the same attitude of mind toward each other that Christ Jesus had, so that with one mind and one voice you may glorify the God and Father of our Lord Jesus Christ.

MATTHEW 18:20

"For where two or three gather in my name, there am I with them."

GALATIANS 3:28

You are all one in Christ Jesus.

1 THESSALONIANS 3:9

How can we thank God enough for you in return for all the joy we have in the presence of our God because of you?

1 THESSALONIANS 3:12

May the Lord make your love increase and overflow for each other and for everyone else, just as ours does for you.

1 PETER 1:22

Now that you have purified yourselves by obeying the truth so that you have sincere love for each other, love one another deeply, from the heart.

EXCELLENCE

GENESIS 18:19

"For I have chosen him, so that he will direct his children and his household after him to keep the way of the LORD by doing what is right and just."

ZECHARIAH 8:13

"So I will save you, and you will be a blessing. Do not be afraid, but let your hands be strong."

JEREMIAH 15:19

"If you repent, I will restore you that you may serve me."

MATTHEW 4:19

"Come, follow me," Jesus said, "and I will send you out to fish for people."

JOHN 14:12

"Very truly I tell you, whoever believes in me will do the works I have been doing, and they will do even greater things than these, because I am going to the Father."

1 TIMOTHY 1:12

I thank Christ Jesus our Lord, who has given me strength, that he considered me trustworthy, appointing me to his service.

PSALM 101:6

My eyes will be on the faithful in the land, that they may dwell with me; the one whose walk is blameless will minister to me.

REVELATION 1:6

And has made us to be a kingdom and priests to serve his God and Father — to him be glory and power for ever and ever! Amen.

MATTHEW 20:26–28

"Whoever wants to become great among you must be your servant, and whoever wants to be first must be your slave — just as the Son of Man did not come to be served, but to serve, and to give his life as a ransom for many."

JOHN 15:8

This is to my Father's glory, that you bear much fruit, showing yourselves to be my disciples.

1 CORINTHIANS 12:4–5

There are different kinds of gifts, but the same Spirit distributes them. There are different kinds of service, but the same Lord.

PEACE

ROMANS 5:1–2

Therefore, since we have been justified through faith, we have peace with God through our Lord Jesus Christ, through whom we have gained access by faith into this grace in which we now stand.

EXODUS 33:14

"My Presence will go with you, and I will give you rest."

PSALM 85:8

I will listen to what God the LORD says; he promises peace to his people, his faithful servants.

PSALM 119:165

Great peace have those who love your law, and nothing can make them stumble.

ISAIAH 26:3

You will keep in perfect peace those whose minds are steadfast, because they trust in you.

ISAIAH 57:2

Those who walk uprightly enter into peace; they find rest as they lie in death.

ISAIAH 32:17

The fruit of that righteousness will be peace; its effect will be quietness and confidence forever.

MATTHEW 11:29

"Take my yoke upon you and learn from me, for I am gentle and humble in heart, and you will find rest for your souls."

EPHESIANS 2:14

He himself is our peace.

COLOSSIANS 3:15

Let the peace of Christ rule in your hearts, since as members of one body you were called to peace. And be thankful.

JOHN 14:27

"Peace I leave with you; my peace I give you. I do not give to you as the world gives. Do not let your hearts be troubled and do not be afraid."

NUMBERS 6:24–26

"The LORD bless you and keep you; the LORD make his face shine on you and be gracious to you; the LORD turn his face toward you and give you peace."

JOY

JOHN 16:24

Until now you have not asked for anything in my name. Ask and you will receive, and your joy will be complete.

PSALM 68:3

May the righteous be glad and rejoice before God; may they be happy and joyful.

PSALM 90:14

Satisfy us in the morning with your unfailing love, that we may sing for joy and be glad all our days.

PSALM 16:11

You make known to me the path of life; you will fill me with joy in your presence, with eternal pleasures at your right hand.

JOHN 15:10–11

"If you keep my commands, you will remain in my love, just as I have kept my Father's commands and remain in his love. I have told you this so that my joy may be in you and that your joy may be complete."

ISAIAH 51:11

Everlasting joy will crown their heads. Gladness and joy will overtake them, and sorrow and sighing will flee away.

HEBREWS 12:2

Fixing our eyes on Jesus, the pioneer and perfecter of faith. For the joy set before him he endured the cross, scorning its shame.

JOHN 16:22

You will rejoice, and no one will take away your joy.

NEHEMIAH 8:10

"The joy of the LORD is your strength."

PSALM 97:11

Light shines on the righteous and joy on the upright in heart.

ROMANS 15:13

May the God of hope fill you with all joy and peace as you trust in him, so that you may overflow with hope by the power of the Holy Spirit.

1 PETER 1:8

Though you have not seen him, you love him; and even though you do not see him now, you believe in him and are filled with an inexpressible and glorious joy.

ENCOURAGEMENT

1 PETER 2:9

You are a chosen people, a royal priesthood, a holy nation, God's special possession, that you may declare the praises of him who called you out of darkness into his wonderful light.

PSALM 138:8

The LORD will vindicate me; your love, LORD, endures forever — do not abandon the works of your hands.

DEUTERONOMY 10:12

And now, Israel, what does the LORD your God ask of you but to fear the LORD your God, to walk in obedience to him, to love him, to serve the LORD your God with all your heart and with all your soul.

JEREMIAH 29:11

"For I know the plans I have for you," declares the LORD, "plans to prosper you and not to harm you, plans to give you hope and a future."

2 THESSALONIANS 2:16–17

May our Lord Jesus Christ himself and God our Father, who loved us and by his grace gave us eternal encouragement and good hope, encourage your hearts and strengthen you in every good deed and word.

HEBREWS 6:10

God is not unjust; he will not forget your work and the love you have shown him as you have helped his people and continue to help them.

MATTHEW 5:16

Let your light shine before others, that they may see your good deeds and glorify your Father in heaven.

TITUS 3:8

I want you to stress these things, so that those who have trusted in God may be careful to devote themselves to doing what is good. These things are excellent and profitable for everyone.

1 PETER 4:11

If anyone speaks, they should do so as one who speaks the very words of God. If anyone serves, they should do so with the strength God provides, so that in all things God may be praised through Jesus Christ.

HEAVEN

ZECHARIAH 2:10

"Shout and be glad, Daughter Zion. For I am coming, and I will live among you," declares the LORD.

COLOSSIANS 3:4

When Christ, who is your life, appears, then you also will appear with him in glory.

HEBREWS 9:28

Christ was sacrificed once to take away the sins of many; and he will appear a second time, not to bear sin, but to bring salvation to those who are waiting for him.

HEBREWS 10:37

"He who is coming will come and will not delay."

1 Thessalonians 4:16–17

The Lord himself will come down from heaven, with a loud command, with the voice of the archangel and with the trumpet call of God, and the dead in Christ will rise first. After that, we who are still alive and are left will be caught up together with them in the clouds to meet the Lord in the air. And so we will be with the Lord forever.

John 14:2–3

"My Father's house has many rooms; if that were not so, would I have told you that I am going there to prepare a place for you? And if I go and prepare a place for you, I will come back and take you to be with me that you also may be where I am."

Acts 1:11

"Men of Galilee," they said, "why do you stand here looking into the sky? This same Jesus, who has been taken from you into heaven, will come back in the same way you have seen him go into heaven."

1 John 3:2

We know that when Christ appears, we shall be like him, for we shall see him as he is.

Revelation 1:7

"Look, he is coming with the clouds," and "every eye will see him, even those who pierced him."

Matthew 24:44

Be ready, because the Son of Man will come at an hour when you do not expect him.

_____EVERLASTING LIFE_____

John 6:40

"For my Father's will is that everyone who looks to the Son and believes in him shall have eternal life, and I will raise them up at the last day."

2 Corinthians 4:14

The one who raised the Lord Jesus from the dead will also raise us with Jesus and present us with you to himself.

Philippians 3:20–21

But our citizenship is in heaven. And we eagerly await a Savior from there, the Lord Jesus Christ, who, by the power that enables him to bring everything under his control, will transform our lowly bodies so that they will be like his glorious body.

Job 19:25–27

"I know that my redeemer lives, and that in the end he will stand on the earth. And after my skin has been destroyed, yet in my flesh I will see God; I myself will see him with my own eyes — I, and not another."

Isaiah 26:19

But your dead will live, Lord; their bodies will rise — let those who dwell in the dust wake up and shout for joy.

1 Corinthians 15:51–52

We will not all sleep, but we will all be changed . . . the dead will be raised imperishable, and we will be changed.

Romans 6:5

If we have been united with him in a death like his, we will certainly also be united with him in a resurrection like his.

Psalm 17:15

When I awake, I will be satisfied with seeing your likeness.

Hosea 13:14

"I will deliver this people from the power of the grave; I will redeem them from death. Where, O death, are your plagues? Where, O grave, is your destruction?"

John 5:25

"The dead will hear the voice of the Son of God and those who hear will live."

PART TWO

❖

GOD'S PROMISES WHEN YOU ARE IN NEED

Scripture speaks confidently. God loves you deeply, and he will meet all your needs. At times you have emotional need, and God's Word brings calm. At times you need guidance, and his Word gives counsel. At times God works directly through circumstances or Christian brothers and sisters. Whatever the situation, God will provide comfort, counsel and peace.

DOUBT

1 JOHN 4:15

If anyone acknowledges that Jesus is the Son of God, God lives in them and they in God.

PSALM 34:22

The LORD will rescue his servants; no one who takes refuge in him will be condemned.

ROMANS 4:25

He was delivered over to death for our sins and was raised to life for our justification.

ROMANS 9:16

It does not, therefore, depend on human desire or effort, but on God's mercy.

PSALM 130:7

With the LORD is unfailing love and with him is full redemption.

JOHN 11:25–26

Jesus said . . . "I am the resurrection and the life. The one who believes in me will live, even though they die; and whoever lives by believing in me will never die."

ROMANS 3:23–24

All have sinned and fall short of the glory of God, and all are justified freely by his grace through the redemption that came by Christ Jesus.

MATTHEW 9:13

"But go and learn what this means: 'I desire mercy, not sacrifice.' For I have not come to call the righteous, but sinners."

JOHN 1:12

Yet to all who did receive him, to those who believed in his name, he gave the right to become children of God.

ROMANS 4:5

To the one who does not work but trusts God who justifies the ungodly, their faith is credited as righteousness.

JOHN 3:18

Whoever believes in him is not condemned.

JOHN 20:31

These are written that you may believe that Jesus is the Messiah, the Son of God, and that by believing you may have life in his name.

_____GUILT_____

1 CORINTHIANS 6:11

You were washed, you were sanctified, you were justified in the name of the Lord Jesus Christ and by the Spirit of our God.

EPHESIANS 3:12

In him and through faith in him we may approach God with freedom and confidence.

NEHEMIAH 9:17

"You are a forgiving God, gracious and compassionate, slow to anger and abounding in love."

PSALM 130:3–4

If you, LORD, kept a record of sins, Lord, who could stand? But with you there is forgiveness.

2 SAMUEL 14:14

"Like water spilled on the ground, which cannot be recovered, so we must die. But that is not what God desires; rather, he devises ways so that a banished person does not remain banished from him."

ISAIAH 43:25

"I, even I, am he who blots out your transgressions, for my own sake, and remembers your sins no more."

DANIEL 9:9

"The Lord our God is merciful and forgiving, even though we have rebelled against him."

ISAIAH 55:7

Let the wicked forsake their ways and the unrighteous their thoughts. Let them turn to the LORD, and he will have mercy on them.

PSALM 32:2

Blessed is the one whose sin the LORD does not count against them.

JEREMIAH 33:8

"I will cleanse them from all the sin they have committed against me and will forgive all their sins of rebellion against me."

JEREMIAH 3:12–13

" 'I will frown on you no longer, for I am faithful,' declares the LORD, 'I will not be angry forever. Only acknowledge your guilt.' "

JOHN 3:18

Whoever believes in him is not condemned.

FAILURE

EXODUS 14:13

"Do not be afraid. Stand firm and you will see the deliverance the LORD will bring you today."

ISAIAH 41:10

"So do not fear, for I am with you; do not be dismayed, for I am your God. I will strengthen you and help you; I will uphold you with my righteous right hand."

1 CORINTHIANS 4:3–5

I do not even judge myself . . . It is the Lord who judges me. Therefore judge nothing before the appointed time; wait until the Lord comes. He will bring to light what is hidden in darkness and will expose the motives of the heart. At that time each will receive their praise from God.

1 SAMUEL 16:7

"The LORD does not look at the things people look at. People look at the outward appearance, but the LORD looks at the heart."

1 CORINTHIANS 15:58

Therefore, my dear brothers and sisters, stand firm. Let nothing move you. Always give yourselves fully to the work of the Lord, because you know that your labor in the Lord is not in vain.

HEBREWS 10:36

You need to persevere so that when you have done the will of God, you will receive what he has promised.

ISAIAH 33:6

He will be the sure foundation for your times, a rich store of salvation and wisdom and knowledge.

ROMANS 14:4

Who are you to judge someone else's servant? To their own master, servants stand or fall. And they will stand, for the Lord is able to make them stand.

JOSHUA 1:9

"Have I not commanded you? Be strong and courageous. Do not be afraid; do not be discouraged, for the LORD your God will be with you wherever you go."

NEED

1 CHRONICLES 29:11

"Yours, LORD, is the greatness and the power and the glory and the majesty and the splendor, for everything in heaven and earth is yours. Yours, LORD, is the kingdom; you are exalted as head over all."

PSALM 107:9

He satisfies the thirsty and fills the hungry with good things.

PHILIPPIANS 4:19

God will meet all your needs according to the riches of his glory in Christ Jesus.

PSALM 111:5

He provides food for those who fear him.

2 CORINTHIANS 9:10–11

Now he who supplies seed to the sower and bread for food will also supply and increase your store of seed and will enlarge the harvest of your righteousness. You will be enriched in every way so that you can be generous on every occasion, and through us your generosity will result in thanksgiving to God.

PSALM 72:12

He will deliver the needy who cry out, the afflicted who have no one to help.

PROVERBS 28:19

Those who work their land will have abundant food.

ACTS 4:34–35

There were no needy persons among them. For from time to time those who owned land or houses sold them, brought the money from the sales and put it at the apostles' feet, and it was distributed to anyone who had need.

PSALM 37:16

Better the little that the righteous have than the wealth of many wicked.

ISAIAH 11:4

With righteousness he will judge the needy, with justice he will give decisions for the poor of the earth.

PSALM 69:33

The LORD hears the needy.

_____FEAR_____

HEBREWS 13:6

So we say with confidence, "The Lord is my helper; I will not be afraid. What can mere mortals do to me?"

DEUTERONOMY 7:21

Do not be terrified by them, for the LORD your God, who is among you, is a great and awesome God.

1 CHRONICLES 16:25–26

For great is the LORD and most worthy of praise; he is to be feared above all gods. For all the gods of the nations are idols, but the LORD made the heavens.

JEREMIAH 15:20

"I am with you to rescue and save you."

ISAIAH 41:10

"So do not fear, for I am with you; do not be dismayed, for I am your God. I will strengthen you and help you; I will uphold you with my righteous right hand."

PROVERBS 16:7

When the LORD takes pleasure in anyone's way, he causes their enemies to make peace with them.

ISAIAH 35:4

Say to those with fearful hearts, "Be strong, do not fear; your God will come."

2 CORINTHIANS 1:10

He will deliver us.

PHILIPPIANS 4:9

Whatever you have learned or received or heard from me, or seen in me — put it into practice. And the God of peace will be with you.

NEHEMIAH 4:14

"Don't be afraid of them. Remember the Lord, who is great and awesome."

PSALM 28:7

The LORD is my strength and my shield; my heart trusts in him, and he helps me. My heart leaps for joy, and with my song I praise him.

DEUTERONOMY 1:17

"Do not be afraid of anyone, for judgment belongs to God."

JOEL 3:16

The LORD will be a refuge for his people.

PSALM 4:8

In peace I will lie down and sleep, for you alone, LORD, make me dwell in safety.

PSALM 56:3

When I am afraid, I put my trust in you.

ANXIETY

MATTHEW 11:28

"Come to me, all you who are weary and burdened, and I will give you rest."

JOHN 16:33

"I have told you these things, so that in me you may have peace. In this world you will have trouble. But take heart! I have overcome the world."

GENESIS 28:15

"I am with you and will watch over you wherever you go, and I will bring you back to this land. I will not leave you until I have done what I have promised you."

JOB 34:12

"It is unthinkable that God would do wrong, that the Almighty would pervert justice."

PSALM 20:7

Some trust in chariots and some in horses, but we trust in the name of the LORD our God.

PSALM 50:15

"Call on me in the day of trouble; I will deliver you, and you will honor me."

PSALM 55:22

Cast your cares on the LORD and he will sustain you.

PSALM 86:7

When I am in distress, I call to you, because you answer me.

ISAIAH 41:13

"I am the LORD your God who takes hold of your right hand and says to you, Do not fear; I will help you."

PROVERBS 3:5–6

Trust in the LORD with all your heart and lean not on your own understanding; in all your ways submit to him, and he will make your paths straight.

ISAIAH 40:11

He tends his flock like a shepherd: He gathers the lambs in his arms and carries them close to his heart; he gently leads those that have young.

PSALM 68:19

Praise be to the Lord, to God our Savior, who daily bears our burdens.

_____ LONGING _____

PSALM 145:19

He fulfills the desires of those who fear him; he hears their cry and saves them.

2 THESSALONIANS 1:11

We constantly pray for you, that our God may make you worthy of his calling, and that by his power he may bring to fruition your every desire for goodness and your every deed prompted by faith.

PSALM 119:37

Turn my eyes away from worthless things; preserve my life according to your word.

PROVERBS 16:3

Commit to the LORD whatever you do, and he will establish your plans.

PHILIPPIANS 4:12–13

I know what it is to be in need, and I know what it is to have plenty. I have learned the secret of being content in any and every situation, whether well fed or hungry, whether living in plenty or in want. I can do all this through him who gives me strength.

PSALM 84:11

For the LORD God is a sun and shield; the LORD bestows favor and honor; no good thing does he withhold from those whose walk is blameless.

PROVERBS 16:9

In their hearts humans plan their course, but the LORD establishes their steps.

PSALM 16:2

I say to the LORD, "You are my Lord; apart from you I have no good thing."

PROVERBS 28:19

Those who work their land will have abundant food.

JOHN 6:35

Jesus declared, "I am the bread of life. Whoever comes to me will never go hungry, and whoever believes in me will never be thirsty."

MICAH 4:2

"He will teach us his ways, so that we may walk in his paths."

_____DEPRESSION_____

MATTHEW 5:4

"Blessed are those who mourn, for they will be comforted."

EXODUS 33:19

"I will cause all my goodness to pass in front of you, and I will proclaim my name, the LORD, in your presence. I will have mercy on whom I will have mercy, and I will have compassion on whom I will have compassion."

ROMANS 5:5

Hope does not put us to shame, because God's love has been poured out into our hearts through the Holy Spirit, who has been given to us.

JEREMIAH 31:13

"Then young women will dance and be glad, young men and old as well. I will turn their mourning into gladness; I will give them comfort and joy instead of sorrow."

ISAIAH 49:15

"I will not forget you!"

ROMANS 15:13

May the God of hope fill you with all joy and peace as you trust in him, so that you may overflow with hope by the power of the Holy Spirit.

DEUTERONOMY 31:8

"The LORD himself goes before you and will be with you; he will never leave you nor forsake you. Do not be afraid; do not be discouraged."

PSALM 30:5

Weeping may stay for the night, but rejoicing comes in the morning.

ISAIAH 54:8

"With everlasting kindness I will have compassion on you."

ISAIAH 35:10

Everlasting joy will crown their heads. Gladness and joy will overtake them, and sorrow and sighing will flee away.

ROMANS 5:2

Through whom we have gained access by faith into this grace in which we now stand. And we boast in the hope of the glory of God.

PSALM 119:76

May your unfailing love be my comfort, according to your promise to your servant.

PSALM 42:11

Why, my soul, are you downcast? Why so disturbed within me? Put your hope in God, for I will yet praise him, my Savior and my God.

CONFUSION

PHILIPPIANS 1:9–10

This is my prayer: that your love may abound more and more in knowledge and depth of insight, so that you may be able to discern what is best and may be pure and blameless.

JOHN 8:12

"I am the light of the world. Whoever follows me will never walk in darkness, but will have the light of life."

JAMES 1:5

If any of you lacks wisdom, you should ask God, who gives generously to all without finding fault, and it will be given to you.

PSALM 86:11

Teach me your way, LORD, that I may rely on your faithfulness; give me an undivided heart, that I may fear your name.

JEREMIAH 31:9

I will lead them beside streams of water on a level path where they will not stumble.

JEREMIAH 10:23

LORD, I know that people's lives are not their own; it is not for them to direct their steps.

PSALM 32:8

I will instruct you and teach you in the way you should go; I will counsel you with my loving eye on you.

1 CORINTHIANS 2:15–16

The person with the Spirit makes judgments about all things, but such a person is not subject to merely human judgments, for, "Who has known the mind of the Lord so as to instruct him?" But we have the mind of Christ.

LUKE 12:12

"The Holy Spirit will teach you at that time what you should say."

PSALM 16:7

I will praise the LORD, who counsels me; even at night my heart instructs me.

PSALM 119:130

The unfolding of your words gives light; it gives understanding to the simple.

PSALM 119:18

Open my eyes that I may see wonderful things in your law.

PERSECUTION

MATTHEW 5:10

"Blessed are those who are persecuted because of righteousness, for theirs is the kingdom of heaven."

GENESIS 50:20

"You intended to harm me, but God intended it for good to accomplish what is now being done, the saving of many lives."

2 SAMUEL 22:4

"I called to the LORD, who is worthy of praise, and have been saved from my enemies."

PSALM 16:8

I keep my eyes always on the LORD. With him at my right hand, I will not be shaken.

PSALM 32:10

Many are the woes of the wicked, but the LORD's unfailing love surrounds the one who trusts in him.

PSALM 37:1–2

Do not fret because of those who are evil or be envious of those who do wrong; for like the grass they will soon wither, like green plants they will soon die away.

PSALM 103:6

The LORD works righteousness and justice for all the oppressed.

JEREMIAH 20:13

Sing to the LORD! Give praise to the LORD! He rescues the life of the needy from the hands of the wicked.

1 PETER 3:11–12

"They must turn from evil and do good; they must seek peace and pursue it. For the eyes of the Lord are on the righteous and his ears are attentive to their prayer."

ISAIAH 49:25

"I will contend with those who contend with you, and your children I will save."

PSALM 125:3

The scepter of the wicked will not remain over the land allotted to the righteous.

ISAIAH 16:4

The oppressor will come to an end.

_____TEMPTATION_____

1 CORINTHIANS 10:13

God is faithful; he will not let you be tempted beyond what you can bear. But when you are tempted, he will also provide a way out so that you can endure it.

GALATIANS 5:16

Walk by the Spirit, and you will not gratify the desires of the flesh.

JOB 23:10

"He knows the way that I take; when he has tested me, I will come forth as gold."

PSALM 119:104

I gain understanding from your precepts; therefore I hate every wrong path.

JAMES 1:13–14

When tempted, no one should say, "God is tempting me." For God cannot be tempted by evil, nor does he tempt anyone; but each person is tempted when they are dragged away by their own evil desire and enticed.

PSALM 141:4

Do not let my heart be drawn to what is evil so that I take part in wicked deeds along with those who are evildoers; do not let me eat their delicacies.

JOSHUA 23:14

"You know with all your heart and soul that not one of all the good promises the LORD your God gave you has failed. Every promise has been fulfilled; not one has failed."

PROVERBS 10:16

The wages of the righteous is life, but the earnings of the wicked are sin and death.

ISAIAH 48:17

"I am the LORD your God, who teaches you what is best for you, who directs you in the way you should go."

DEUTERONOMY 4:40

Keep his decrees and commands, which I am giving you today, so that it may go well with you and your children after you.

PSALM 119:2

Blessed are those who keep his statutes.

_____SHAME_____

LUKE 12:8

"Whoever publicly acknowledges me before others, the Son of Man will also acknowledge before the angels of God."

LUKE 15:10

"There is rejoicing in the presence of the angels of God over one sinner who repents."

PSALM 40:10

I do not hide your righteousness in my heart; I speak of your faithfulness and your saving help. I do not conceal your love and your faithfulness from the great assembly.

EZEKIEL 36:23

Then the nations will know that I am the LORD . . . when I am proved holy through you before their eyes.

JOHN 13:35

"By this everyone will know that you are my disciples, if you love one another."

1 PETER 3:14–16

"Do not fear their threats; do not be frightened." But in your hearts revere Christ as Lord. Always be prepared to give an answer to everyone who asks you to give the reason for the hope that you have. But do this with gentleness and respect.

ROMANS 1:16

I am not ashamed of the gospel, because it is the power of God that brings salvation to everyone who believes.

ACTS 20:26–27

"I declare to you today that I am innocent of the blood of any of you. For I have not hesitated to proclaim to you the whole will of God."

ROMANS 10:15

"How beautiful are the feet of those who bring good news!"

JOHN 15:26–27

"When the Advocate comes, whom I will send to you from the Father — the Spirit of truth who goes out from the Father — he will testify about me. And you also must testify."

IMPATIENCE

1 PETER 3:1

Wives, in the same way submit yourselves to your own husbands so that, if any of them do not believe the word, they may be won over without words by the behavior of their wives.

ACTS 16:31

"Believe in the Lord Jesus, and you will be saved — you and your household."

1 Corinthians 7:13–14

If a woman has a husband who is not a believer and he is willing to live with her, she must not divorce him. For the unbelieving husband has been sanctified through his wife, and the unbelieving wife has been sanctified through her believing husband. Otherwise your children would be unclean, but as it is, they are holy.

John 1:41–42

The first thing Andrew did was to find his brother Simon and tell him, "We have found the Messiah" (that is, the Christ). And he brought him to Jesus.

Ezekiel 18:21–23

"If a wicked person turns away from all the sins they have committed and keeps all my decrees and does what is just and right, that person will surely live; they will not die. None of the offenses they have committed will be remembered against them. Because of the righteous things they have done, they will live. Do I take any pleasure in the death of the wicked? declares the Sovereign Lord. Rather, am I not pleased when they turn from their ways and live?"

Proverbs 22:6

Start children off on the way they should go, and even when they are old they will not turn from it.

2 Peter 3:9

The Lord is not slow in keeping his promise, as some understand slowness. Instead he is patient with you, not wanting anyone to perish, but everyone to come to repentance.

Isaiah 54:13

"All your children will be taught by the Lord."

SUFFERING

ROMANS 5:3–4

Not only so, but we also glory in our sufferings, because we know that suffering produces perseverance; perseverance, character; and character, hope.

1 PETER 3:14

If you should suffer for what is right, you are blessed. "Do not fear their threats; do not be frightened."

1 PETER 5:10

The God of all grace, who called you to his eternal glory in Christ, after you have suffered a little while, will himself restore you and make you strong, firm and steadfast.

PSALM 71:20

Though you have made me see troubles, many and bitter, you will restore my life again.

JOB 2:10

"Shall we accept good from God, and not trouble?"

1 PETER 4:12–13

Dear friends, do not be surprised at the fiery ordeal that has come on you to test you, as though something strange were happening to you. But rejoice inasmuch as you participate in the sufferings of Christ, so that you may be overjoyed when his glory is revealed.

ISAIAH 25:8

The Sovereign LORD will wipe away the tears from all faces.

PSALM 34:19

The righteous person may have many troubles, but the LORD delivers him from them all.

ISAIAH 50:10

Let the one who walks in the dark, who has no light, trust in the name of the LORD and rely on their God.

1 PETER 2:20–21

If you suffer for doing good and you endure it, this is commendable before God. To this you were called, because Christ suffered for you, leaving you an example, that you should follow in his steps.

ISAIAH 42:16

"I will lead the blind by ways they have not known, along unfamiliar paths I will guide them; I will turn the darkness into light before them and make the rough places smooth. These are the things I will do; I will not forsake them."

WEAKNESS

PSALM 142:3

When my spirit grows faint within me, it is you who watch over my way.

PSALM 147:6

The LORD sustains the humble but casts the wicked to the ground.

ISAIAH 57:15

"I live in a high and holy place, but also with the one who is contrite and lowly in spirit, to revive the spirit of the lowly and to revive the heart of the contrite."

HABAKKUK 3:19

The Sovereign LORD is my strength; he makes my feet like the feet of a deer, he enables me to tread on the heights.

1 CHRONICLES 16:11

Look to the LORD and his strength; seek his face always.

PSALM 37:10–11

A little while, and the wicked will be no more; though you look for them, they will not be found. But the meek will inherit the land and enjoy peace.

PSALM 55:18

He rescues me unharmed from the battle waged against me, even though many oppose me.

PSALM 62:11

One thing God has spoken, two things I have heard: "Power belongs to you, God."

PSALM 72:13

He will take pity on the weak and the needy and save the needy from death.

2 CORINTHIANS 12:9

"My grace is sufficient for you, for my power is made perfect in weakness." Therefore I will boast all the more gladly about my weaknesses, so that Christ's power may rest on me.

JEREMIAH 10:6

No one is like you, LORD; you are great, and your name is mighty in power.

EPHESIANS 3:16

I pray that out of his glorious riches he may strengthen you with power through his Spirit in your inner being.

_____ DEJECTION _____

HEBREWS 4:15–16

We do not have a high priest who is unable to empathize with our weaknesses, but we have one who has been tempted in every way, just as we are — yet he did not sin. Let us then approach God's throne of grace with confidence, so that we may receive mercy and find grace to help us in our time of need.

JEREMIAH 29:13

"You will seek me and find me when you seek me with all your heart."

JEREMIAII 33:3

"Call to me and I will answer you and tell you great and unsearchable things you do not know."

ISAIAH 65:24

"Before they call I will answer; while they are still speaking I will hear."

ROMANS 8:26–27

The Spirit helps us in our weakness. We do not know what we ought to pray for, but the Spirit himself intercedes for us through wordless groans. And he who searches our hearts knows the mind of the Spirit, because the Spirit intercedes for God's people in accordance with the will of God.

DANIEL 9:18

"We do not make requests of you because we are righteous, but because of your great mercy."

JAMES 4:8

Come near to God and he will come near to you.

PSALM 86:5

You, Lord, are forgiving and good, abounding in love to all who call to you.

JEREMIAH 24:7

I will give them a heart to know me, that I am the LORD. They will be my people, and I will be their God, for they will return to me with all their heart.

PSALM 145:10

All your works praise you, LORD; your faithful people extol you.

_____DESPAIR_____

HAGGAI 2:4

"Be strong, all you people of the land," declares the LORD, "and work. For I am with you."

JAMES 1:12

Blessed is the one who perseveres under trial because, having stood the test, that person will receive the crown of life that the Lord has promised to those who love him.

EZEKIEL 34:16

I will search for the lost and bring back the strays. I will bind up the injured and strengthen the weak.

ISAIAH 40:29

He gives strength to the weary and increases the power of the weak.

ISAIAH 51:6

My salvation will last forever, my righteousness will never fail.

DANIEL 2:23

"I thank and praise you, God of my ancestors: You have given me wisdom and power."

2 THESSALONIANS 3:3

The Lord is faithful, and he will strengthen you and protect you from the evil one.

HEBREWS 10:35

Do not throw away your confidence; it will be richly rewarded.

JEREMIAH 32:17

"Ah, Sovereign LORD, you have made the heavens and the earth by your great power and outstretched arm. Nothing is too hard for you."

EPHESIANS 1:18

I pray that the eyes of your heart may be enlightened in order that you may know the hope to which he has called you.

PSALM 46:1

God is our refuge and strength, an ever-present help in trouble.

PSALM 119:116

Sustain me, my God, according to your promise, and I will live; do not let my hopes be dashed.

PSALM 100:5

For the LORD is good and his love endures forever; his faithfulness continues through all generations.

ISAIAH 51:5

"My salvation is on the way."

_____ANGER_____

JAMES 4:10

Humble yourselves before the Lord, and he will lift you up.

PSALM 73:25–26

Whom have I in heaven but you? And earth has nothing I desire besides you. My flesh and my heart may fail, but God is the strength of my heart and my portion forever.

EZEKIEL 36:26

"I will give you a new heart and put a new spirit in you."

ISAIAH 2:17–18

The arrogance of man will be brought low and human pride humbled.

EPHESIANS 4:26–27

"In your anger do not sin": Do not let the sun go down while you are still angry, and do not give the devil a foothold.

PSALM 141:5

My prayer will still be against the deeds of evildoers.

JAMES 1:19–20

Everyone should be quick to listen, slow to speak and slow to become angry, because human anger does not produce the righteousness that God desires.

Philippians 2:3

Do nothing out of selfish ambition or vain conceit. Rather, in humility value others above yourselves.

Galatians 5:22–23

The fruit of the Spirit is love, joy, peace, forbearance, kindness, goodness, faithfulness, gentleness and self-control.

Psalm 86:15

But you, Lord, are a compassionate and gracious God, slow to anger, abounding in love and faithfulness.

Proverbs 17:13

Evil will never leave the house of one who pays back evil for good.

DISAPPOINTMENT

Psalm 62:8

Trust in him at all times, you people; pour out your hearts to him, for God is our refuge.

John 15:7

If you remain in me and my words remain in you, ask whatever you wish, and it will be done for you.

James 4:2–3

You desire but do not have, so you kill. You covet but you cannot get what you want, so you quarrel and fight. You do not have because you do not ask God. When you ask, you do not receive, because you ask with wrong motives, that you may spend what you get on your pleasures.

Psalm 145:18

The Lord is near to all who call on him, to all who call on him in truth.

Romans 8:28

In all things God works for the good of those who love him, who have been called according to his purpose.

PSALM 10:17

You, LORD, hear the desire of the afflicted; you encourage them, and you listen to their cry.

MATTHEW 18:19

"If two of you on earth agree about anything they ask for, it will be done for them by my Father in heaven."

PSALM 66:18–19

If I had cherished sin in my heart, the Lord would not have listened; but God has surely listened and has heard my prayer.

PSALM 33:18

But the eyes of the LORD are on those who fear him, on those whose hope is in his unfailing love.

MARK 11:24

"Whatever you ask for in prayer, believe that you have received it, and it will be yours."

EPHESIANS 3:20

Now to him who is able to do immeasurably more than all we ask or imagine, according to his power that is at work within us.

PSALM 31:14

But I trust in you, LORD.

GRIEF

ISAIAH 43:2

"When you pass through the waters, I will be with you."

PSALM 116:15

Precious in the sight of the LORD is the death of his faithful servants.

1 THESSALONIANS 4:13–14

Brothers and sisters, we do not want you to be uninformed about those who sleep in death, so that you do not grieve like the rest of mankind, who have no hope. For we believe that Jesus died and rose again, and so we believe that God will bring with Jesus those who have fallen asleep in him.

PSALM 10:14

But you, God, see the trouble of the afflicted; you consider their grief and take it in hand. The victims commit themselves to you; you are the helper of the fatherless.

REVELATION 21:3–4

"God himself will be with them and be their God. 'He will wipe every tear from their eyes. There will be no more death' or mourning or crying or pain, for the old order of things has passed away."

PSALM 71:20–21

Though you have made me see troubles, many and bitter, you will restore my life again; from the depths of the earth you will again bring me up. You will increase my honor and comfort me once more.

JOHN 14:3

"If I go and prepare a place for you, I will come back and take you to be with me that you also may be where I am."

PSALM 119:28

My soul is weary with sorrow; strengthen me according to your word.

PSALM 119:50

My comfort in my suffering is this: Your promise preserves my life.

PSALM 119:76

May your unfailing love be my comfort, according to your promise to your servant.

DISOBEDIENCE

LUKE 11:28

"Blessed . . . are those who hear the word of God and obey it."

JOHN 7:17

"Anyone who chooses to do the will of God will find out whether my teaching comes from God or whether I speak on my own."

JOHN 15:10

"If you keep my commands, you will remain in my love, just as I have kept my Father's commands and remain in his love."

JAMES 1:25

Whoever looks intently into the perfect law that gives freedom, and continues in it — not forgetting what they have heard, but doing it — they will be blessed in what they do.

1 JOHN 2:5

If anyone obeys his word, love for God is truly made complete in them. This is how we know we are in him.

MATTHEW 7:24

"Everyone who hears these words of mine and puts them into practice is like a wise man who built his house on the rock."

PSALM 119:35

Direct me in the path of your commands, for there I find delight.

MATTHEW 16:27

"For the Son of Man is going to come in his Father's glory with his angels, and then he will reward each person according to what they have done."

JOHN 14:23

"Anyone who loves me will obey my teaching. My Father will love them, and we will come to them and make our home with them."

PSALM 128:1

Blessed are all who fear the LORD, who walk in obedience to him.

JOHN 8:31–32

Jesus said, "If you hold to my teaching, you are really my disciples. Then you will know the truth, and the truth will set you free."

PSALM 119:67

Now I obey your word.

_____NEGLECT_____

EXODUS 19:5–6

" 'Now if you obey me fully and keep my covenant, then out of all nations you will be my treasured possession. Although the whole earth is mine, you will be for me a kingdom of priests and a holy nation.' These are the words you are to speak to the Israelites."

EPHESIANS 2:10

We are God's handiwork, created in Christ Jesus to do good works, which God prepared in advance for us to do.

1 CORINTHIANS 12:14–18,22

The body is not made up of one part but of many. Now if the foot should say, "Because I am not a hand, I do not belong to the body," it would not for that reason stop being part of the body. And if the ear should say, "Because I am not an eye, I do not belong to the body," it would not for that reason stop being part of the body. If the whole body were an eye, where would the sense of hearing be? If the whole body were an ear, where would the sense of smell be? But in fact God has placed the parts in the body, every one of them, just as he wanted them to be . . . On the contrary, those parts of the body that seem to be weaker are indispensable.

LUKE 9:48

"Whoever welcomes this little child in my name welcomes me; and whoever welcomes me welcomes the one who sent me. For it is the one who is least among you all who is the greatest."

1 Corinthians 3:8–9

The one who plants and the one who waters have one purpose, and they will each be rewarded according to their own labor. For we are co-workers in God's service.

James 1:27

Religion that God our Father accepts as pure and faultless is this: to look after orphans and widows in their distress and to keep oneself from being polluted by the world.

1 Peter 3:10–11

"Whoever would love life and see good days must keep their tongue from evil and their lips from deceitful speech. They must turn from evil and do good."

SICKNESS

Psalm 73:26

My flesh and my heart may fail, but God is the strength of my heart and my portion forever.

Jeremiah 33:6

"Nevertheless, I will bring health and healing to it; I will heal my people and will let them enjoy abundant peace and security."

James 5:14–15

Is anyone among you sick? Let them call the elders of the church to pray over them and anoint them with oil in the name of the Lord. And the prayer offered in faith will make the sick person well; the Lord will raise them up.

Jeremiah 17:14

Heal me, Lord, and I will be healed; save me and I will be saved, for you are the one I praise.

Psalm 23:4

Even though I walk through the darkest valley, I will fear no evil, for you are with me; your rod and your staff, they comfort me.

Exodus 23:25–26

"Worship the LORD your God, and his blessing will be on your food and water. I will take away sickness from among you, and none will miscarry or be barren in your land. I will give you a full life span."

Psalm 30:2

LORD my God, I called to you for help, and you healed me.

Psalm 41:3

The LORD sustains them on their sickbed and restores them from their bed of illness.

Psalm 119:76

May your unfailing love be my comfort, according to your promise to your servant.

Psalm 3:3

But you, LORD, are a shield around me, my glory, the One who lifts my head high.

Isaiah 57:18

"I have seen their ways, but I will heal them; I will guide them and restore comfort to Israel's mourners."

UNCERTAINTY

James 5:8

You too, be patient and stand firm, because the Lord's coming is near.

Psalm 27:13–14

I remain confident of this: I will see the goodness of the LORD in the land of the living. Wait for the LORD; be strong and take heart and wait for the LORD.

Isaiah 30:15

"In repentance and rest is your salvation, in quietness and trust is your strength, but you would have none of it."

PSALM 37:34

Hope in the LORD and keep his way. He will exalt you to inherit the land; when the wicked are destroyed, you will see it.

JAMES 5:7–8

Be patient, then, brothers and sisters, until the Lord's coming. See how the farmer waits for the land to yield its valuable crop, patiently waiting for the autumn and spring rains. You too, be patient and stand firm.

REVELATION 1:9

The suffering and kingdom and patient endurance ... are ours in Jesus.

PROVERBS 19:11

A person's wisdom yields patience.

ISAIAH 40:31

Those who hope in the LORD will renew their strength. They will soar on wings like eagles; they will run and not grow weary, they will walk and not be faint.

ROMANS 2:7

To those who by persistence in doing good seek glory, honor and immortality, he will give eternal life.

PSALM 37:7

Be still before the LORD and wait patiently for him; do not fret when people succeed in their ways, when they carry out their wicked schemes.

1 TIMOTHY 1:16

I was shown mercy so that in me, the worst of sinners, Christ Jesus might display his immense patience as an example for those who would believe in him and receive eternal life.

FRUSTRATION

MATTHEW 5:7

"Blessed are the merciful, for they will be shown mercy."

PHILIPPIANS 2:4

Not looking to your own interests but each of you to the interests of the others.

1 CORINTHIANS 13:5

[Love] does not dishonor others, it is not self-seeking, it is not easily angered, it keeps no record of wrongs.

JAMES 4:11–12

Brothers and sisters, do not slander one another. Anyone who speaks against a brother or sister or judges them speaks against the law and judges it. When you judge the law, you are not keeping it, but sitting in judgment on it. There is only one Lawgiver and Judge, the one who is able to save and destroy. But you — who are you to judge your neighbor?

1 PETER 4:8

Above all, love each other deeply, because love covers over a multitude of sins.

1 JOHN 5:16

If you see any brother or sister commit a sin that does not lead to death, you should pray.

EPHESIANS 4:31–32

Get rid of all bitterness, rage and anger, brawling and slander, along with every form of malice. Be kind and compassionate to one another, forgiving each other, just as in Christ God forgave you.

PSALM 141:3

Set a guard over my mouth, LORD; keep watch over the door of my lips.

PSALM 37:8–9

Refrain from anger and turn from wrath; do not fret — it leads only to evil. For those who are evil will be destroyed, but those who hope in the LORD will inherit the land.

MATTHEW 18:15

"If your brother or sister sins, go and point out their fault, just between the two of you. If they listen to you, you have won them over."

2 THESSALONIANS 1:6–7

God . . . will pay back trouble to those who trouble you and give relief to you who are troubled.

_____INSECURITY_____

ROMANS 10:1

Brothers and sisters, my heart's desire and prayer to God . . . is that they may be saved.

JOHN 17:11

"Holy Father, protect them by the power of your name, the name you gave me, so that they may be one as we are one."

HEBREWS 13:18

Pray for us. We are sure that we have a clear conscience and desire to live honorably in every way.

EPHESIANS 1:17

I keep asking that the God of our Lord Jesus Christ, the glorious Father, may give you the Spirit of wisdom and revelation, so that you may know him better.

EPHESIANS 1:18–19

I pray that . . . you may know the hope to which he has called you, the riches of his glorious inheritance in his holy people, and his incomparably great power for us who believe.

EPHESIANS 3:17–19

I pray that you . . . may have power, together with all the Lord's holy people, to grasp how wide and long and high and deep is the love of Christ, and to know this love that surpasses knowledge — that you may be filled to the measure of all the fullness of God.

EPHESIANS 6:19

Pray also for me, that whenever I speak, words may be given me so that I will fearlessly make known the mystery of the gospel.

PHILIPPIANS 1:9–11

This is my prayer: that your love may abound more and more in knowledge and depth of insight, so that you may be able to discern what is best and may be pure and blameless for the day of Christ, filled with the fruit of righteousness that comes through Jesus Christ — to the glory and praise of God.

COLOSSIANS 3:16

Let the message of Christ dwell among you richly as you teach and admonish one another with all wisdom through psalms, hymns, and songs from the Spirit, singing to God with gratitude in your hearts.

PART THREE

YOUR PRAYERS ... GOD'S ANSWERS

The Bible contains many prayers uttered by God's people. These prayers serve as models for us, helping us to express ourselves to the Lord. Scripture is also rich in promises that give us a foretaste of God's answers to our prayers. We may not know when or how God will answer when we cry out to him. But we do know that he hears us, and that he will do what is good for us.

_____YOUR PRAYER . . . GOD'S ANSWER_____

P: MATTHEW 6:9–13

"This, then, is how you should pray: 'Our Father in heaven, hallowed be your name, your kingdom come, your will be done, on earth as it is in heaven. Give us today our daily bread. And forgive us our debts, as we also have forgiven our debtors. And lead us not into temptation, but deliver us from the evil one.'"

A: PSALM 47:8

God reigns over the nations; God is seated on his holy throne.

DANIEL 2:44

"The God of heaven will set up a kingdom that will never be destroyed."

DANIEL 7:27

"Then the sovereignty, power and greatness of all the kingdoms under heaven will be handed over to the holy people of the Most High. His kingdom will be an everlasting kingdom, and all rulers will worship and obey him."

PSALM 111:5

He provides food for those who fear him; he remembers his covenant forever.

JEREMIAH 33:8

"I will cleanse them from all the sin they have committed against me and will forgive all their sins of rebellion against me."

JAMES 1:13

God cannot be tempted by evil, nor does he tempt anyone.

1 JOHN 4:4

You, dear children, are from God and have overcome them, because the one who is in you is greater than the one who is in the world.

P: PSALM 140:1

Rescue me, LORD, from evildoers; protect me from the violent.

A: PROVERBS 29:25

Fear of man will prove to be a snare, but whoever trusts in the LORD is kept safe.

P: PSALM 141:10

Let the wicked fall into their own nets, while I pass by in safety.

A: PROVERBS 14:14

The faithless will be fully repaid for their ways, and the good rewarded for theirs.

P: PSALM 90:15

Make us glad for as many days as you have afflicted us, for as many years as we have seen trouble.

A: JOEL 2:25

"I will repay you for the years the locusts have eaten."

P: PSALM 68:28

Summon your power, God; show us your strength, our God, as you have done before.

A: ISAIAH 49:8

"In the time of my favor I will answer you, and in the day of salvation I will help you."

P: PSALM 51:1–2

Have mercy on me, O God, according to your unfailing love; according to your great compassion blot out my transgressions. Wash away all my iniquity and cleanse me from my sin.

A: PSALM 103:12

As far as the east is from the west, so far has he removed our transgressions from us.

P: PSALM 143:2

Do not bring your servant into judgment, for no one living is righteous before you.

A: PSALM 145:8

The LORD is gracious and compassionate, slow to anger and rich in love.

P: JEREMIAH 31:18

"I have been disciplined. Restore me, and I will return, because you are the LORD my God."

A: HEBREWS 12:14

Make every effort to live in peace with everyone and to be holy; without holiness no one will see the Lord.

P: PSALM 119:66

Teach me knowledge and good judgment, for I trust your commands.

A: JOHN 13:17

"Now that you know these things, you will be blessed if you do them."

P: PSALM 119:10

I seek you with all my heart; do not let me stray from your commands.

A: EZEKIEL 36:27

"I will put my Spirit in you and move you to follow my decrees and be careful to keep my laws."

P: DANIEL 9:19

"Lord, listen! Lord, forgive! Lord, hear and act! For your sake, my God, do not delay."

A: HOSEA 14:4

"I will heal their waywardness and love them freely, for my anger has turned away from them."

P: PSALM 143:8

Let the morning bring me word of your unfailing love, for I have put my trust in you. Show me the way I should go, for to you I entrust my life.

A: MATTHEW 5:18

"For truly I tell you, until heaven and earth disappear, not the smallest letter, not the least stroke of a pen, will by any means disappear from the Law until everything is accomplished."

P: PSALM 140:9

Those who surround me proudly rear their heads; may the mischief of their lips engulf them.

A: ISAIAH 13:11

I will punish the world for its evil, the wicked for their sins.

P: PSALM 10:12

Arise, LORD! Lift up your hand, O God. Do not forget the helpless.

A: MICAH 5:4

He will stand and shepherd his flock in the strength of the LORD, in the majesty of the name of the LORD his God. And they will live securely, for then his greatness will reach to the ends of the earth.

P: PSALM 38:18

I confess my iniquity; I am troubled by my sin.

A: JEREMIAH 3:22

"Return, faithless people; I will cure you of backsliding."

P: PSALM 7:9

Bring to an end the violence of the wicked and make the righteous secure — you, the righteous God who probes minds and hearts.

A: PSALM 96:13

He will judge the world in righteousness and the peoples in his faithfulness.

P: PSALM 143:10

Teach me to do your will, for you are my God; may your good Spirit lead me on level ground.

A: DEUTERONOMY 30:19–20

I have set before you life and death, blessings and curses. Now choose life . . . love the LORD your God, listen to his voice, and hold fast to him. For the LORD is your life.

P: PSALM 51:12

Restore to me the joy of your salvation and grant me a willing spirit, to sustain me.

A: DEUTERONOMY 28:9

The LORD will establish you as his holy people, as he promised you on oath, if you keep the commands of the LORD your God and walk in obedience to him.

P: PSALM 69:29

But as for me, afflicted and in pain — may your salvation, God, protect me.

A: PSALM 68:20

Our God is a God who saves.

P: PSALM 5:8

Lead me, LORD, in your righteousness because of my enemies — make your way straight before me.

A: JOHN 3:21

Whoever lives by the truth comes into the light.

P: PSALM 22:11

Do not be far from me, for trouble is near and there is no one to help.

A: ZECHARIAH 8:8

"I will be faithful and righteous to them as their God."

P: Psalm 25:7

Do not remember the sins of my youth and my rebellious ways; according to your love remember me, for you, Lord, are good.

A: Jeremiah 15:19

"If you repent, I will restore you that you may serve me."

P: Psalm 71:9

Do not cast me away when I am old; do not forsake me when my strength is gone.

A: Psalm 92:14–15

They will still bear fruit in old age, they will stay fresh and green, proclaiming, "The Lord is upright."

P: Psalm 90:12

Teach us to number our days, that we may gain a heart of wisdom.

A: Revelation 2:10

Be faithful, even to the point of death, and I will give you life as your victor's crown.

P: Psalm 25:16

Turn to me and be gracious to me, for I am lonely and afflicted.

A: Jeremiah 32:41

"I will rejoice in doing . . . good."

P: Psalm 70:4

May all who seek you rejoice and be glad in you; may those who long for your saving help always say, "The Lord is great!"

A: Psalm 145:7

They celebrate your abundant goodness and joyfully sing of your righteousness.

P: Psalm 60:5

Save us and help us with your right hand, that those you love may be delivered.

A: Psalm 64:9

All people will fear; they will proclaim the works of God and ponder what he has done.

P: Psalm 39:12

"Hear my prayer, Lord, listen to my cry for help."

A: Psalm 6:9

The Lord has heard my cry for mercy; the Lord accepts my prayer.

EXPRESSIONS OF PRAISE

Psalm 89:2

I will declare that your love stands firm forever, that you have established your faithfulness in heaven itself.

Psalm 35:10

My whole being will exclaim, "Who is like you, Lord?"

Psalm 57:9–10

I will praise you, Lord, among the nations; I will sing of you among the peoples. For great is your love, reaching to the heavens; your faithfulness reaches to the skies.

Psalm 59:16

I will sing of your strength, in the morning I will sing of your love; for you are my fortress, my refuge in times of trouble.

Psalm 59:17

You are my strength, I sing praise to you; you, God, are my fortress, my God on whom I can rely.

Psalm 61:8

I will ever sing in praise of your name and fulfill my vows day after day.

PSALM 63:4

I will praise you as long as I live, and in your name I will lift up my hands.

PSALM 63:7

Because you are my help, I sing in the shadow of your wings.

PSALM 66:20

Praise be to God, who has not rejected my prayer or withheld his love from me!

1 TIMOTHY 1:17

Now to the King eternal, immortal, invisible, the only God, be honor and glory for ever and ever. Amen.

DEUTERONOMY 32:3–4

I will proclaim the name of the LORD. Oh, praise the greatness of our God! He is the Rock, his works are perfect, and all his ways are just. A faithful God who does no wrong, upright and just is he.

PSALM 89:8

Who is like you, LORD God Almighty? You, LORD, are mighty, and your faithfulness surrounds you.

PSALM 92:5

How great are your works, LORD, how profound your thoughts!

PSALM 104:33

I will sing to the LORD all my life; I will sing praise to my God as long as I live.

PSALM 18:1

I love you, LORD, my strength.

PSALM 139:14

I praise you because I am fearfully and wonderfully made; your works are wonderful, I know that full well.

PSALM 145:3

Great is the LORD and most worthy of praise; his greatness no one can fathom.

ISAIAH 12:1

"I will praise you, LORD. Although you were angry with me, your anger has turned away and you have comforted me."

JEREMIAH 32:18–19

"Great and mighty God, whose name is the LORD Almighty, great are your purposes and mighty are your deeds."

PSALM 68:35

You, God, are awesome in your sanctuary; the God of Israel gives power and strength to his people. Praise be to God!

LUKE 1:46

"My soul glorifies the Lord."

PSALM 89:1–2

I will sing of the LORD's great love forever; with my mouth I will make your faithfulness known through all generations. I will declare that your love stands firm forever, that you have established your faithfulness in heaven itself.

REVELATION 4:11

"You are worthy, our Lord and God, to receive glory and honor and power, for you created all things, and by your will they were created and have their being."

PSALM 107:1

Give thanks to the LORD, for he is good; his love endures forever.

_____YOUR FAVORITE VERSES_____

_____YOUR FAVORITE VERSES_____

_____YOUR FAVORITE VERSES_____

_____YOUR FAVORITE VERSES_____

Also available in the DayBreak series:

DayBreak Prayers for Believers Hardcover: 9780310421528

DayBreak Promises from Proverbs Hardcover: 9780310421542

DayBreak Verses for Men Hardcover: 9780310421498

DayBreak Verses for Women Hardcover: 9780310421504

Available in stores and online!